SEEKING THE HOOK

New & Selected Poems
by
Lou Lipsitz

SIGNAL BOOKS

Chapel Hill, NC

illustrations by Philip Kuznicki
cover design by Michael Brown
design production by Cassio Lynm
cover photograph by Steve Bly
author photograph by Willa Stein

For information or to order copies of this book write:

Signal Books
P.O. Box 16534
Chapel HIll, NC 27516

Or call:

(919) 870-9849

For Annie
For Jon
In memory of Bud's songs

Acknowledgements

NEW POEMS
These poems appeared (sometimes in slightly different versions) in the following books and periodicals:

Antaeus: "Leaving the Psychiatrist's Office"
Caliban: "The Wolf," "The Forest is Burning...,"
   "Why the Poet Reads First..."
Cardinal: "Ten Warnings in Search..."
Inroads: "Dreamless Night"
Kansas Quarterly: "Hungarian Aunts"
The Literary Review: "Throwing Away Several Pages of
   Poetry"
New American Review: "On the death of Jack Lipsitz"
New Letters: "Separation," "Song of the Divorced
   Father"
The New Republic: "Brooklyn Summer"
Nimrod: "The Grief," "The Dugout"
Northwest Poetry Review: "Why the Dodgers Never
   Left Brooklyn"
Pembroke Magazine: "Poignant Moment...,"
   "Anthropology," "Dealing with the fact..."
Poetry East: "Root"
Southern Poetry Review: "Dream: Initiation,"
   "Betty Adcock tells me....,"
   "Birth of the Bear Clan," "Word"
Southern Review: "Old Self," "Seeking the Hook"
St. Andrews Review: "Autumn Evening"
The Sun: "Sperm," "Anniversary of My Father's

Death," "Inner Family," "Jealousy," "Gangster
Song," "To S. after years apart"
University of South California Anthology, 1988: "Blackberry
Authorities"
Witness: "King Kong," "Against Literature"
Young American Poets: "For WGF..."

SELECTED POEMS

Some poems have been revised.

Cold Water, Wesleyan University Press, Middletown, Ct.,
1967

Reflections On Samson, kayak press, Santa Cruz, Ca., 1977

Contents

SELECTED POEMS

Reflections On Samson

Cold Water

New Poems

Part 1

Seeking The Hook

with its barbed point digging
into the soft palate behind my lower teeth
I am dragged along the mud and rock-strewn
bottom for forty feet, then pulled up
drawn toward the light as I twist and
yank my head side to side and the hook
lodges deeper in my mouth I taste
the blood a silent cry goes up through
my skull and it is all so quick I see
the surface a hand the light overwhelms
me, and I lunge a last time with the hook
ripping across my lips and I'm free
suddenly falling back gasping through
air then slipping beneath the surface
into the dim, green sweetness and
the flesh of my mouth throbbing water
flowing through me and yet slowly,
beyond thought or even the will
to survive, I feel myself turn and
go back, seeking the hook and it
is there again, waiting for me,
rigid and tiny, the hidden barb
like a beautiful lie, too powerful
for me to resist, so that later when
they lift me, strip me, tear my guts
out and present me cooked and
spread open, I will believe I am being
honored like a new king.

Middle-Aged Man Experiences Spring

Spring is the spongy dough
being shaped from mud and leaves
kneaded over and over by practiced hands.

I walk slower. I'm not trying to get very far.
Like the top of a convertible, an inner eye
is drawn back.

I lie down on the new grass of the park.
My heart thuds slow and hard
like a heavyweight who dances away
then punches the big bag.

When I get home, the door will be opened
like a stove. I'll be baked into four
brown rolls and eaten at dinner. Afterwards,
we'll open the windows to let out the light.

It's good to have two hands: one
for each universe.

Gangster Song

he's got a woman
      with lovely tits
so small and sweet
    he can't take his hands
    out of her blouse

they're in the convertible
tooling
    through town, top down,
the gangster's
    wearing a bright green shirt
the color of money
when it's happy

the poker game
    is as good as won
      sitting at the table
    he inhales
    a cigarette
and the smoke
    pours through his nostrils
slow, like a locomotive
pulling into the station

when he gets home
    he scratches
      his son's back
beautifully

in smooth, even strokes,
        with his large
sleepy nails

    O what happened,
                he sings,
        what happened
to the ache
it was supposed
            to be to live?

Blackberry Authorities

When I first came out to the country
    I knew nothing. I watched
as people planted, harvested, picked
    the berries, explained
the weather, tended the ducks and horses.

When I first came out to the country
    my mind emptied and I
liked it that way. My mind was like a sky
    without clouds, a summer sky
with several birds flapping across a field
    on the eastern horizon.

I liked the slowness of things. The empty
    town, the lake stillness,
the man I met who seemed contented, who
    sat and talked in the dusk
about why he had chosen this long ago.

I did better dreaming then. the colors
    were clear. I found something
important in myself: capacity for renewal.
    And at night, the sky so intense.
Clear incredible stars! Almost another earth.

But now I see there are judgments here.
    This way of planting or that.
The arguments about fertilizers and organics;

            problems of time, figuring how
to allocate what we have. So many matters
            to fasten on and dissect.

That's the way it is with revelations.
            If you live it out, you start
thinking, examining. The mind cries out
            for materials to play with.
Right now, in fact, I'm excited about
            several new vines and waiting
for the blackberry authorities to arrive.

The Dugout

I'm learning a kind of skill
a delicacy in handling despair

it's like the earth
that absorbs and absorbs
and turns and grows endlessly
and dies

fires burn through ten forests
huge pressures squeeze down
on so much carbon and
preserve it, fuse it. there are substances
under the surface no one knows
about and they go on evolving

there will always be sleep
and it will always be troubled
there will always be love
and it will rise and tumble
and subside like the ocean currents

the dugout carved from a cedar tree
and rowed by sixteen men
strokes along the inner river
and the rain falls steadily, like
grief, that we need for the deep,
heavy forests and the marsh
where the nests are.

Thirteen Ways of Looking at a Mattress

"I was of three minds,
Like a tree
In which there are three blackbirds."

Wallace Stevens

1

You can turn
away from the mattress
and turn slowly
toward it again
and it will still
be there.

2

The mattress hangs
on a wall. You
lean against it, your
hair already
starting to dream.

3

I've been told
they carried the mattress
far down
in the hold of
an old ship, like

a sail that had grown
too fat to fly.

4

There was no
place for the darkness
and the winter
clouds to descend.
Therefore
they came to
inhabit the mattress.

5

At times, I have
to say I am of
tres azules — like
the memory
of an apartment
with three
extinct mattresses.

6

We carried it up
the stairs over
our heads. At
the third floor

11

a small boy appeared
upon it
and spoke to us,
bewilderingly, in
an unknown language.

7

Can't you detect
the odor of wine?
Sleeping
on the mattress, I
can see again the
genie who lived
in the bottle.

8

In certain counties, the
birds, feverish
for change, tried
futilely to carry
the mattress into
the trees.

9

I don't know which
I hate more:
the pain of actual
effort, or the anticipation

of it. Getting
out of bed, or
knowing I have to.

10

To resolve the old dilemma:
No, you cannot
remove the pea from
beneath the mattress.
You must make
a home within the pod.

11

It seemed I lay
back on the mattress
and slipped into
a nest of sticks
and ashes —
and there was still
some warmth.

12

No one knows we
slept here. And no one
cares either.
We are crazy and have
been up too long
looking for

a sunrise
through the mattress.

13

The mattress is
nothing. But
will we ever finish
the stories
we have to tell
about it?

The Grief

The grief spreads like red wine
    knocked over on the tablecloth by the drunk father

It's a highschoolgirl's hair
    that gets in my mouth — the girl who scorned me
    twenty years ago

And I get mad and want to poke somebody
    and I drive crazy on the highway
    and yell at various people unknown to me

The grief spreads into my sleep
    it climbs down the ladder from the roof
    and slips in the window and lies down
    beside me with its twig fingers

It continues like the second day of rain
    and the third day and the confusion about buying
    something trivial and the memory
    I can't remember exactly that won't leave me alone

I'm down on my knees with a rag
    for some reason trying to wipe up puddles
    and I'm laughing way inside that at least
    I've forgotten what that girl's hair tastes like

Now's the moment though when I want to buy time
    but they won't take my money.

Unlove

300 yards ahead
        the dog stood in the road

my high beams glittered
        for a second in its eyes

I flicked the lights
        up and down to warn her
blew the horn twice
        my foot still on the gas
and the dog trotted
        to the right, then stopped,
looked toward me again
        now an instant away

        70mph, narrow country
        road, 2am

        and she turned
back into the road, turned
        looking at the lights
and swerving
        I hit her.
She lay there, motionless,
        thrown onto the shoulder
probably dead, a brown dog
        with long legs. I was afraid
to touch her. The two of us

infinite and tiny in the enormous
darkness and the headlight beams.
    I walked away, drove on
thinking I would be haunted
    I would dream of the dog
and my impatience, my clear
    inexcusable certainty; the dog
would be crossing
    this road in my memory
and my sleepy right foot would
    this time hit the brake
and the huge, jolting car
    would halt. Everything
safe.

At 2:30 am you were asleep:
    the one I'd rushed home for —
cheeks flushed, athletic body
    stretched across the sheet,
one knee pulled up to your breasts
    like an insignia of longing —
all the torment
    gone out of your face.

Why didn't I see then
    that nothing would break
our momentum;
    that we would lie finally

by the road, headlights
　　　blazing white on our silent bodies —
the howl never risen from our throats?

King Kong

The simplicity
    she's lying on the ground
    waiting for you

O Kong, natural force,
    stirrer of bays and rivers with your mighty legs
    tosser of boulders that echo
    down the valley for miles

O Kong, weird lonely monarch,
    she's yours — reward for all those years
    of living alone and cursing your origins

And no need to talk to her. No need
to explain your desire, discuss
the latest movies. No need
to open your heart like a pomegranate
and have her bite the little sour seeds.

Instead, you will lift her toward you
in the palm of your hand
    and she will cling to your finger
as the wind of your power
    blows across her body. She will
pull the burrs from your hair
    and comb your comical ears.
Finally, you'll place her gently
    on the ground

and roll her over with your tongue
like in a caterpillar
        in its gorilla cocoon.

O amiable possessor, what then?
Your huge gorilla prick
        just won't fit inside her
        it's impossible!

Can you dream then
        that she grows to your size
or that for one hazardous night
        you shrink to our vulnerable state?
Or is this why
        poetry was invented?

Jealousy

the man you went with
the man with hair that seemed
to lean toward the past

with so much
red-gold
left in his beard

the man you went with
who got you to laugh so
often at his other language
that seemed
entirely original

with the strange
clear eyes who just shook his head
gently

the man you went with
who taught you to listen
and forget

now I take you in my arms
and he is here with us
I look into his eyes
I reach out to touch his hands
I realize I've loved him
all my life.

Seeking Sleep

Hey — they turned the moon off!
    gone by my window
        once too often

I stick my arm out
and get a glassful of dark air.
O to pour
    the night over my head!
O for a taste
    of nothing!
    Everything I've lost —
years gone into the past's
shoes.
Now for the other life!
        the one
without mistakes.

I finally dream of you.
I'm like a mountain goat
searching for your window
as my crazy hooves
clack along the deserted
streets of town.

Ten Warnings for Men

"Beware of the man who praises liberated women;
he is planning to quit his job."

Erica Jong, *"Seventeen Warnings*
in Search of A Feminist Poem"

Beware of the woman poet;
she's waiting to be surprised by a swan.

Beware of the woman with sharp pencils;
she thinks you're a marginal note.

Beware of the woman who keeps coming toward you;
she thinks she's the light at the end of the tunnel.

Beware of the woman who accepts you as you are;
she's weary.

Beware of the woman who loves to cook;
she'll make you delve into the leftovers.

Beware of the woman who won't cook;
she'll eat you raw.

Beware of the woman who won't be touched;
she keeps a list of small injuries.

Beware of the woman who lifts weights;
she'll let you down.

Beware of the unliberated woman;
she knows when to call her lawyer.

Beware of the liberated woman;
she's her own lawyer.

Betty Adcock tells me there are 1,086 meanings of
the word "romantic"

at first this was hard to believe, but once she
had reached number 29 i knew
    we were in for a major afternoon.
as that meaning required
    i took the hand of a seemingly sweet
    young woman on my left and skipped a full half
mile through spring gardens almost forgetting
Betty was still working on the list

rushing back, she'd come to #100,
    and i felt the breath of tragedy sweep by me
    like a bus exhaust. i fell down
on the busy sidewalk and was repeatedly
trampled by hordes of unfeeling busy people
    who preferred to continue
on their respective ways and not consider
    the beauty hidden beneath the mask
of my infirmities.

at meaning #215 i ran up the stairs into
    my childhood house and embraced my mother
    who was busy preparing the meatloaf
and who smelled of onions and paprika, an aroma
that has haunted me all my life
    whenever i touch a woman's belly.

by the time i got outside again, having
        stopped to consume a plate of meatloaf
and potatoes
        Betty had gotten up to meaning #784
which involved the enthusiastic, even desperate
plunging naked
        into a country lake which contained
somewhere in or on its muddy bottom a rare object
—coin, jewel, or whatever— that had been tossed
        there by the incredibly beautiful — WOW —
mysterious woman who was watching, idly, on
        the opposite shore and she too
quite naked.

 i never found it, but wet,
        with muddy feet and a bit
tired, i returned as Betty
        arrived at the final meaning
number 1,086: a spontaneous inner
        vibration that
lifts one slowly but surely
        off the face of this
complicated earth because of the perception
of a resonance with all Nature
        clouds included.
Bye Betty, i waved
        from the top
    of a local oak
Bye Betty
        Bye.

Sperm

Spit
from the lips of God

hot and sticky
drenched with

eternity's
equatorial softness

the milky come
spurts out —

my prick is only
the passageway

the drawbridge over
which these

thrashing messengers
travel, bursting forth

like marathon runners
shouldering each other

at the start of the race
bringing their ancient

information that
the war

is over that we
survived

that no one
can deny our

history that parts of
all the ones

who came before
us crowd into

this room around
our bed — Yes,

it's cramped
but who ever said

evolution was going
to be comfortable?

I make out half a lip in
the crooked smile

of one of my Russian
forebears, who stands

far in the back, keeping
a portion of his fur

overcoat on.

Against "Literature": After opening at random
a newly published book of poems

"I fall upon the thorns of life. I bleed."

Shelley

"A book should be the ax for the frozen sea inside us."

Kafka

The sophisticated ManhattanPoet looks out in 1980 (over the
pretentiously efficient glass and steel workboxes of our dubi-
ous urban civilization) at dusk, and writes that the descend-
ing sun, the familiar darkening red sphere reminds him of a
stag-poor creature with a spike near its heart, chased down
by those redcoated guys on horseback, dogs yelping. It's an
evening in New York City and where did that image come
from? Literature, of course.

But the trouble is, this guy's never seen a stag outside a zoo
though he's been to a few of those outdated stag parties with
the girl in the cake and the tanked-up margarita drinkers
and the poor bridegroom pissing out a window onto the
white shirt of a passerby who thinks — My God! the damn
rain has turned yellow in this stupid city. And the poet
knows he should have stopped writing sometime back, got-
ten on with life without the comfort of placing words neatly
on a page — captive words — with no power of their own.
They can't get up and drive home when the party's dull.
They're stuck in the sad zoo of literature.

We're too unromantic these days for the poet to blurt out:
"I'm like the stag you see, kind of, and I'm (have you
noticed?) dripping a little over here..." The laughter would be
too much, and besides, it's a lie. He doesn't bleed any more
than lots of others — except, what is it...higher quality
blood? Nonetheless, the poet broods, anxious like the patient
in the dentist's chair about to get the injection, or the wel-
fare family waiting for the third eviction notice. He broods at
sunset and that's when the stag comes to him, hunted down
and bleeding. The stag comes and saves him with its literary
death. Because life aches and real poetry also aches and
something has to stop it.

But this is not the way the poet sees it. He figures he'll soon
be on the phone. They're planning a party at somebody's
estate. All this year's trendy artists will be there and the
place will be dripping with significance like a jumbo shrimp
in cocktail sauce. That's what literature is anyway, isn't it: a
paté you can taste over and over in the house of impor-
tance? Where you can at last enjoy chasing your own tail,
shooting arrows at your shadow; where you can stagger out
across the vast lawn of traditions at dusk and fail to recog-
nize the coming dark for what it is — something that's been
around a couple of billion years.

A Man Confused After Lovemaking

*"...sex has to contain a man's entire emotional
vocabulary."*

Daphne Kingma

I didn't know how to explain
so I attempted to make love to you.
It didn't work well.
I came too fast.
Blood pounded in my head.

I only wanted to escape the old
livingroom.
Escape, but also hold onto its peculiar
dimness and have you continue
to follow me.

To follow me? or just to wonder
who I was?
And who were you really?
My sister in some way; my mother
who had created and hidden
the absence?

And what did I want really?
To appear and disappear like a firefly?
To put my head in your lap?
To play the elusive chess game with
crumbling pieces?
Or to break into the party, crush a few things
and throw all the dancers to the floor?

The sign language of the body stutters
— a few incomprehensible syllables —
      outcries — frozen like a mammoth.

Word

Looking at my right hand, I can imagine
picking up the heavy, black, cast-iron skillet
and lifting it quietly off the stove.
Her back is turned. I raise the skillet over
her head and smash it down against
her skull. She crumbles, falls toward the floor.
I stand over her, the skillet still poised,
my hand itching to do it again.

No. Instead I locate the word "fool."
A simple word that dances out along
the fingers of my left hand. The word is
a tiny person dressed in a wild costume:
one arm yellow, the other red;
one leg green, the other purple.
He wears a blue cap decorated with
silver stars. His nose is tinted orange.
There are bells on his woven black slippers.
He does somersaults in my hand. He jumps
and shouts. Look how entertaining he is!
I hold him out toward her. He wants to jump
on her shoulder and play with her hair.
O, watch out, he has a little scissors!

Evening

The poet's test
is to write a poem
called "evening"
beginning in the small street
near the bay
where they are selling clams.

There must be a woman
he is pursuing
in his own distracted way
— someone he has sought
for years
and can almost catch.

There must be a fire
somewhere
in the darkening sun for example
or in a room
where logs are flaming
and the poet
must hold back and wait
until he knows
exactly what not to say.

Then, when he opens his lips,
the moon will
come out of his mouth.

Birth of the Bear Clan

*"One day the brothers who had been driven out came
together, killed and devoured their father...After they
had got rid of him...the affection which had all this time
been pushed under was bound to make itself felt...They
revoked their deed by forbidding the killing of the totem."*
                              Sigmund Freud, Totem & Taboo

I have almost stopped remembering how it was
before — how long we waited, how long
I survived his beatings. How long we starved
and huddled together fearing
his powerful blows.
I remember how he beat me for touching the leg
of the red-haired one.
He beat us for talking, for stealing the food.
Sometimes he just drove us out.
Was only he entitled to live, to partake
of the women's bodies?

Yet he too had to sleep, even if the sharp rock
was always under his hand. He also
must dream and his mouth fall open like a cut.
It was not so hard then to take the life from him.
But we were afraid and the first blow failed
to finish him. He rose like a black bear
and howled. Then we hit him
from the other side and he bled and fell.

And we did not turn away. We finished it.
We sent him home to his mother in pieces of blood.
And we tore at his flesh and ate until we
couldn't stand the taste. We are not children
to be beaten, starved and forgotten.

Afterwards, it was as if we were dreaming while
awake. It was as if we had never been born, as if
we had lived forever. Yet sometimes one of us
woke hearing his voice and we felt lost in the dust.

When I look at these females we killed him
for, they do not seem so much: like
this one, a little square-faced and pale,
sitting next to me, hand on my thigh, looking
at me sometimes with that peculiar message.

Sometimes I want to lay down the spear
I have sharpened so long and carefully.
I don't know if I wish to speak or to wait
for someone else to speak, but:
This must never happen again.

We took his bones and placed them
at the north of our encampment. We go each day
and walk around the pile. We chant.
We say again what we did. In the cave,
one of us made a drawing of him, bleeding

and surrounded. We have chosen never
to speak his name. Now we call ourselves
the Bear Clan because the bear is our ally
and we will not descend on him.

Root

Today, after six months here,
I saw
     for the first time, a root,
round and smooth as a hose,
covered with a thin layer
of gray bark
     a solid hickory root I think
that came up out of the earth
and then, two feet farther, went
back into it, like a snake,
appearing and disappearing
at the same time.

That was the way I wanted it
with you: a surfacing — brief
and real, fixed in our memories —
     but when we danced
I couldn't help lifting you
out of the earth.

To S. after Years Apart

Dusk. The horse no one calls
begins to amble home from the fields.

I open the door of time
and breathe the misty, incomparable autumn.

Then I go again to find the old woman
who lives just beyond the turn
in the road. She has a potion
that cures the ailments of love.

Half our lives we've been sick
with a passion that bent our bones
the way a child bends a sapling in play
pulling its leaves to the ground.
By now, nothing can untangle
the branches.

But as I knew, the old woman is gone.
Her house long ago abandoned.
Night will come soon and dark solitude.
I'll sit by the fire and watch
the wood of fate burn. It takes
many years to turn to ash.

Then our confused and inconsolable
passion will twist itself
around my heart like smoke
drifting from the chimney.

Autumn Evening

Girls of fifteen drift across
the landscape like balloons
released at the game.

The stadiums are empty now.
Cars filled with beer, laughter
and foolish emblems have disappeared
into the red dusk.

I stand still and begin to feel
the fortuitous earth spinning;
its twisted rails turned toward
the long angles of darkness.

The forgotten language starts
to come back to me. I remember
that phrase about stars in our belts.
Then I see the old pirate, high
in a tree, looking for the sun,
knife gripped in his teeth.

Throwing Away Several Pages of Poetry

They were decent little nuggets
almost. Interesting lumps of ideas,
I think. Stupid, incoherent, nearly
lovable phrases. A few beginnings
and I tossed them away. threw them
into the invisible heap of rejected things
like a drunk landlord, so sure of himself,
singing Puccini as he goes up the basement
steps after dropping the rent checks
into the coalbin.

Well, now I go back into the basement
to search for them. I've come to
wonder what shadow of things
I was trying to find words for; what
form of love was too trivial or sad
to acknowledge. Naked, I nose
into the coalbin, the fine fur
of coal dust slowly settling over me.
I dig through the hunks of black,
concealed fire, and then I think
suddenly — why am I here? why
couldn't I just forget, just let go,
or why didn't I save everything,
every word, every crazily valued
bent coin of experience? Because,
I hear myself say, there is no
peace, dammit, no real peace.

Why the Poet Always Read First and the Fiction-Writer Second at the Sunday afternoon Readings at the Art School in Carrboro, NC

— for Paul Jones

The reason is that poetry was present
at the poorly advertised
first audition of the Universe
     when a slight breath of cloud
     passed over the dark waters

poetry was in fact that cloud
     which passed effortlessly
     through God's ears

while the ancestors of fiction-writers
took tenthousand centuries
to evolve
     toiling sideways in the primal mud
     on their miniscule legs, gossiping
     intensely of their plots and
     subplots

because poetry came out of the tree
like a bird
     without a nest

because poetry is so close to dance
and therefore swirls and twists even
     if ever so slightly

and allied as well to the music of flutes
and drums recalling certain rituals
for example — two people, a man and a woman,
howling, alternately, in the dark cave

because poetry came out of the tree
very slowly
and then darted right back into it
because the students of ontology
and deontology continue to bow
their heads in disbelief and
cannot make up their minds what
sort of universe this is
but meantime the rock can skip
across the waters
and the sea mammal can rise
out of the deep, snorting and braying,
and so God is probably
a poem, still in the process
of composition by an undeniably talented
but distracted surrealist who was there
in the Garden of Eden and
whispered to Adam: "Isn't that a mango?"

because in the pitchdark
I take off my clothes and stand
in the not-so-sacred woods bathing in
moonlight, waiting for you
perfectly sober, perfectly aware

that what I do
   is destined by the chains of protein
rattling in my cells
and I am locked to the wall of my being
   noisy with pleasure, waiting
to be extinguished

the reason is that this arrangement is
practical. the poet has to leave earlier.
   he has fewer words but those few
   are strangely heavy. so he will unwrap
them a little, let them cry out like an infant
whose discontent
   we cannot figure out. all we know is
sooner or later
   it will sleep
because there is the missing nest,
the bird, the puddle in the rain
   and the branch vibrating with
what is about or not yet about
   to exist.

New Poems

Part 2

On the death of Jack Lipsitz

As to heaven — since he was no saint,
I'm not sure my father was admitted.
He was the sort, you see, not especially
given to taking orders. If God
instructed him to butcher his son,
the way Abraham was told, he would
have hesitated, probably offering
an excuse like an arm gone arthritic,
or, having taken me to the mountain,
would have suffered a case of acute
heartburn and been helped home,
burping.

That night he would have whispered
to me: "What is this, killing my son?
The man must have emotional
problems. I hear also he burns cities
supposedly wicked. He must be under
a strain. You have to overlook sometimes."
And coughing once or twice, would have
fallen asleep.

Had any prophets been around, they
would have preached against his kind.
A man of the belly, they would have said,
giving over his life unto earthly pleasures,
unto suntan and games of chance. A man
never seen in the sanctuaries of the Lord,

but taking himself instead into barbershops,
movies, haberdasherers, and, sometimes,
a casino. They would lament his slavery
to convention. A man without backbone
from the teachings of The Book.

So when he came to The Gate, perhaps
they would have admitted him, grudgingly,
for after all, he had never engaged in
cruelty, had never forgotten entirely how
to love. They would have warned him though
and cautioned him to keep to the side streets,
out of sight of the righteous men and women
who spread their pious, obedient wings
on the main boulevards.

After a couple of weeks, he would have
gone quietly to find the gin rummy players
who live on the outskirts of Hell.

Meeting My Son at the Airport

I'm there before and I wait.
When he comes through the passageway
I remember his being born,
dark-haired infant pushed out
with his mother's blood.
Now he carries the colorful
valise on his shoulder and
doesn't see me. I'm standing
right in front of him and he
doesn't see me. He doesn't
let on that he sees me.

This is the moment it is all
said. You walked out on me, dad.
I won't ever get angry. I won't
even feel the betrayal. You
walked out on us and I was
six years old. Now you come
to the airport and I don't
see you.

For a moment I imagine him
flying at me and knocking me down;
or the two of us, out of breath,
bewildered, on our knees, weeping.
But he walks on, a prince
in gorgeous athletic robes who
stops for no one. And then, as I

reach out for him, he seems
like a blind boy too proud
to ask for help.

I take one of his bags
and hug him. It's done.
Damage of twenty years ago.
If I live long enough and
he returns one day to
the small, locked, forgotten
door and I am allowed to
return from this unacknowledged
exile, maybe we will meet again.

Why the Dodgers Never Left Brooklyn

in the warm takenforgranted room
with a day bed, two chairs, a small table
and some pictures and a mirror,
the boy sits next to his grandfather
who adjusts the radio tuning slightly to
cut down the static and hear
Red Barber more clearly broadcasting
a Dodger nightgame
the score is 3-2 favor the
Phillies, bottom of the eighth
Robin Roberts on the mound
and Jackie Robinson up
runner on second.

in the warm takenforgranted
evening as things unfold slowly
as the windup occurs and Red Barber
conveys that to the boy and
the grandfather, as the pitch
zooms toward the plate and Jackie
has his eye on it, there's
a wonderful tension
in the boy's stomach, almost
an unspoken prayer, a
prayer for victory because
defeat is so painful so thorough
so indescribable. Because the boy
has grown up knowing what

the Dodgers might be, knowing
what Furillo can do, and Campanella,
and Pee Wee Reese. He has seen
Duke Snyder hit the big one and
Billy Cox stop a ball at third
that no one knew could be stopped
by a human being.

and so in the dark in the room
on the day bed next
to his grandfather
the boy knows the feeling
of the takenforgranted hand
that rests quietly
against his own, knows the next
game is Saturday and
the voice of Red Barber will
come through the radio,
knows in the sheltered corridors
of his heart, where the Dodgers
come and go, knocking
dirt from their spikes,
that the team will
never leave Brooklyn.

Poignant Moment, listening to "Lakes" played by
the Pat Metheny Group, Sunset Beach, Summer,
1984

The song comes over me like a wheatfield, my face
    brushed by golden stalks

My spirit moves forward like a blind one and when
    things touch me...I see them

How could I know there was so much tenderness
    hidden in things, in my flesh?

How could I know the love of the white paint for
    the porch of the house where it clings
    and flakes? How could I know my daughter
    would come back?

How could I know about the air or the inquiring,
    efficient blood, returning to the cells?

I see the love of the pale blue wind for our clothes,
    blown out from the line,

The wind loves our house, whistling through tiny
    cracks, blowing steadily toward us.

There is something in me that listens and stirs.
    Everything flows, grasping. Everything is
    a kind of attachment, a music; time aching
    through us.

It is too much to feel. I put down my pad. Even
   breathing is a kind of ceaseless music.

I see we cannot rest, ever. We seek for love,
   continually, carried along like dust, swept
   across lakes. How did I ever come to be
   here, to know these people, to love them?

Our need for love exceeds us, reaching ahead,
   dark hair blowing like a torch in the halls
   of the old castle. It goes ahead, looking
   for signs, listening, searching.

And then the wind catches it suddenly and lifts it,
   swift and beautiful, carries it far out over
   the lakes — sail without a boat, banner
   of our incorrigible longings.

Leaving the Psychiatrist's Office

"Psychology is nothing but a history which persists
in us because we have not been able to rise from it."

                                        Joel Kovel

I sit in the car
          and cry
for twenty minutes

feeling
          it will never stop
there is
          no bottom

          finally
grabbing hold
of myself
          like some new
recruit
          in the marines —

the part of me that judges
the sincerity
          of weeping
says:
          this is the genuine thing
grieving
          over what is gone forever:
          twenty years wasted

the way lost
wandering
through the city
like one of the homeless
carrying rags and stones
in an old orange sack
the energy of a boy
purchased finally
by a chicken dealer
who had him sit by the hour
counting the feathers
on a stuffed bird

and the method that
might have
been simplest:
                    sexual love —
that would come
so slowly, with
certainty, like a
sunrise
        — became so
complicated
— a prism that seared
the eyes, a shadow
thrown this way and that
on the pavement
by a windblown tree —

and something else:
      let's calling it "knowing"
— as the early fog
burned off
and you could see the ocean
there
      enormous and majestic
— the easy waves
of what you wanted to do.

But now, I am like two wrestlers
who fall to the canvas together
locked somehow, their arms
and legs beyond releasing;
their fierce energy focused
like a knot pulled tighter
by trying to undo it;
their crushed dance doomed
to last forever.

"Your mother," the doctor says,
"talk about
your mother." And I am here,
turning gray, years old, 44.

Hungarian Aunts

— *for Dennis Szakacs*

At Thanksgiving, the fat Hungarian aunts
go crazy, filling the tables
with goulash and stuffed cabbage,
with lentil and barley soups the
big crazy aunts whisper in Hungarian
they get out the super-paprika and
pour it into everything because
it makes you live 120 years at least
(if you take care) and then they slice
the secret Hungarian apple that fell
from the Tree of Ignorance and whose
golden flesh has made us as stupid as
we are.

They never get tired, the fat crazy aunts.
In the kitchen they play games, calling
each other Indian names like "Little
Orange Juice Bird" or "Blue Sky Pancake"
and they dance around the kitchen table
like maidens, singing loudly (in Hungarian)
a song about the harvest that was so huge
it burst through the roof.

At Thanksgiving they prepare a turkey also
and the crazy aunts say the bird flew here
from Budapest because that's not so untrue
because really it's not that far from Toledo
is it? say the aunts, grinning, plucking off
the long gray feathers, waving their thick
raw hands, that bleed and harden.

Brooklyn Summer

— for the Friedlands, 1948

She cooked all day
her skin turning rosy
and the walls of the house
seeming to sweat
like heavy leaves in the jungle.

She had a chicken in the oven
even though it was summer
and the open windows
only brought news
of boiling children falling
in the street.

Then, at the end, she
wiped her face, thoughtlessly,
like a swimmer
stepping out of the ocean.

And the father came home
and washed and
my friend Gerry came in
and then they enjoyed
everything, sitting
for an hour sweating
and talking at the table

like guerrillas
who have won the war.

And then, for the first time
in years, she went out
on the fire escape with them
and I heard her laugh
when someone blew smoke rings
and she slept with her foot
hanging over the edge
like a root.

Dream: Initiation

My old father stands beside the used car.
There's a crack in the windshield, streaks of rust.
It's a souped-up Chevy, about '55,
been down the end of a lot of dirt roads.

He looks like a 60-year-old teenager:
white t-shirt, sleeves rolled up, pack
of Luckies tucked in.

He's brought a little blonde for the initiation.
She looks sexy but tough as nails.
Tight jeans and a blouse hanging part open.
Her look says: I won't be easy, but you
can get it if you're man enough.
I'll make your dick feel like a scalded
finger.

He lights a cigarette and stares at me.
He's motioning for me to come along.
My father, who hadn't touched my mother
in 35 years. He's telling me there's nothing
to wait for. Fuck what anybody thinks.
Fuck what you think yourself. Do
what you have to do. What any man
has to do.

Then I open my eyes, erection
in my hand, messenger from the other world.
But my dream father and the little blonde
will wait. One day I will have to come
to her, barrelling along this road
in an old car full of dust and the bitter need
to prove I'm a man.

Old Self

"Many American men...do not have enough awakened or living warriors inside to defend their soul houses."

Robert Bly

I chanced across my old self
today. He was sitting in the second
floor office where I used to work —
at the typewriter, young, thin guy,
in his late 20's, white shirt, narrow
dark tie, serious demeanor, writing
an essay against the Vietnam War.

I came up the stairs and saw him —
a decent human being, diligent,
not remotely aware of the ambush
life had waiting — not knowing
he'd permit himself to be taken
prisoner and then, in confusion,
do desperate things, betray
what he loved — and that nothing
would enable him to survive
as he was.

I passed the open door
and wanted to cry out — warn him,
force the warriors to raise
their spears. But even hearing

my shout, he would have only
hesitated, then turned back to
his devoted, lonely and interminable
work.

Inner Family

*— after being told by the therapist to "live with
my limitations"*

I remember how we called them then: "deaf and
dumb." It was 1950 and Judy's parents lived
in the apartment house at the corner.

Esther, her mother, born deaf, who frightened us
with her efforts at speech — sounds we'd never
heard — like a soft seal's bark.

And Fred, her father, who'd lost his vocal cords
in an accident, who'd smile, gesture to me, shake
his head up and down, acknowledging, then turn
to Esther, touch her hands, explain to her
      while she went on throwing her arms in the air,
a little wild, afraid he didn't understand. And she
would settle down, get in the car. And he would
motion to Judy, as I watched. Judy, who spoke as
we did, but who could flash her hands toward them,
signalling in the other language.

These days I remember the Kaufmans and their
struggles to be understood.
I imagine them driving all day and at night in the
hotel maybe Fred and Esther would caress, write
some love words on each others' palms. And

in the dark Judy might try to listen, imagining
fingers that brush across flesh like the swaying
of large summer leaves.

I remember them in these days because they are
my inner family. They urge me to go on, to gesture,
to live bravely somehow, cheerfully, in this
contorted silence I can never accept.

For WGF who was told he didn't publish enough to
be given tenure

The hell
        with
        universities! For us, long ago, you
were an associate
        professor of liveliness
        who could play
for us
        the music
        we didn't know
            how much we
wanted to hear.

In the journal
            of sweetness
you published
        entire nights! that we will
always
        acknowledge
        in the obscure articles
our hearts
        may write.

Remember teaching us
        about the highland Scots
                of 1746?
— strange determined
        men with
        old loyalties —

marching down from
       their hills
     bagpipes blaring
to be slaughtered on
an open field
     by the modern world's
         artillery?

May they live
     in all of us! But this time
let the Brits
     keep the lowland.
And we'll stay
     in our mountains, preaching
       singing,
          weaving,
     and propagating
     our own
       kind.

Separation

Someone had to decide and so
unable to find another way,
without preparation, with a mix
of acetylene and wound, like someone
in the middle of a highway about
to get smashed, I ran.

I threw some things in a suitcase.
Without explaining. With a few words
to my sixyearold son, with a pat
on the head and some promises, and my
daughter not even there to say goodbye to.

Someone had to do it because I
told myself, she will never take
this blame, and it seemed the last
chance to save myself. And so I walked
away, most alone ever.

Wanting to go back a hundred times, to say
goodbye again, to explain for hours,
to crush them again in my arms, to
apologize again, to be at home a father
again even a husband, to ignore
everything and make believe and hope even
it might be.

But stubbornly I made myself go. I
made myself stay away. I went to the
new apartment and I slept there
trembling alone in a narrow bed like
an auto part in a dusty box, an old
carburetor in a warehouse forgotten
on the waterfront.

Then my son came to visit. Again and again.
It was never enough. Tears withheld that
might ruin our eyes forever. Love and regret
that could tear your arms off. One time he
hit me in the back of the head with a hardball
and I turned and saw the sad fire in his face.
And my daughter couldn't forgive - hurt,
untouchable like someone with a terrible sunburn.
Sometimes she didn't come for weeks.

It all went wrong, I told myself. And now
it's too late. I have nothing and my heart
is sick. Then one day an odd guy snuck into
the room. I'd known him in college, an oboe
player fond of psychology. Remember, he said,
it takes years, and fell asleep.

I can't really breathe, I told him. What
you've lived through is yours, he said.
Then slowly, as he snored, ache in bones,
middleofthenightsadness, subsided.
No longer thoughts of going back.

The days continued to arrive - guests for
some uncertain festivity. One afternoon
I laughed suddenly at a radio show. This
is the new life, I thought, feeling the first
tooth break through my sore baby gums.

The Wolf

— for Jon, who dreamt of him

The wolf knocks at the door.
Father has just gone to
live by himself and now the wolf
comes, carrying a lantern
and wearing a cap of stars.

The wolf knocks but you are afraid.
This is the one they say ate grandmother.
They say he blew down houses.
You hold your breath and hide
under the bed.

When you peek out, you see
his huge teeth, but he has a
tired look. Maybe he has
come far in order to find you.
Does he live secret and alone?
Does he have knowledge
of the directions
fire follows in the blood?

There is a knock at the door.
The wolf's lantern gives off
a blue glow. There is no one
to tell you what to do. He is
wearing a cap of stars.

Trying to deal with the fact that my daughter has
not slept at my house
in 14 years

delicately, delicately,
i offer money to the birds
and bits of birdseed to
the busdriver

i go down to the basement
searching for the autumn
and sit on the chimney
arguing with the worms

there were many words
it seems that might have
been said, but they've been
cancelled, they've dried
and crumbled like plaster

finally i find a hammer
and attack the moon

Song of the Divorced Father

"...I realized that it's inevitable; wounds are part
of what parents give their children."

Michael Meade

There was a woman poet from Chile who
wrote "sleep close to me" to her small son.
Reading that, I think of you, children, now
so long and substantial, now beyond
my picking up and carrying to bed, now
beyond the reach almost of my arms and my soul.

I remember the night silence and my father-ear
listening for your breathing; the cries and
choking sounds that pulled me from sleep.
I remember the early mornings of sentimental
thoughts as I watched your faces utterly
asleep, and then strange dreams you told
of wolves and weddings and curious caves
full of treasure.

Now I want you to sleep near me, to be
in the house with me, so we can sing together
sometimes, so I can relearn your new voices.
So we can carry the wounds together,
pulling them from the sea, an old boat
we used to fish in -

     turn it upsidedown and let the flaking

paint dry in the sun - then when night comes
we can howl and weep - you can hammer me
with your small fists of long ago and we can
hack the boat apart and burn it;
it will burn all night, the stars wheeling above us
as we lie there, separate, exhausted.

Then in the morning, the boat will be intact,
awaiting us, the blue paint fresh. I will say:
"Let's get some fish in the marshes." And you
will steer, knowing the way all over again.

Anthropology

Powerfully lean, skin heated up from thirty minutes
of sprints, Larry wipes his face
on which the beard is just starting to grow.
This is a long time back.

Dedicated runner, considering again and again
the exact way to lean toward the tape,
walking the race out carefully on the cinders,
talking quietly to himself; sixteenyearold
student of physics with delicate hands like
his father's, the thought of killing himself
entered his mind every few days as
something careful, a thoughtful, possible
behavior.

He got home late for dinner and said little.
Were these his people, two talkative boys,
this woman clutching her own hands, asking
where he'd been, the man disguised behind
the newspaper and axiomatic words?
was this the place to learn what it meant
to climb up into the startling caverns of sleep?

What race of people did he belong to,
he wondered. Looking in the mirror, at times
he thought he caught something Indian,
American Indian in the shape of his jaw —

and the eyes were there, scanning distances
from a hidden place.

I dreamt only yesterday he hadn't done it.
He came back from the rocks of the mountain
river and sat with me laughing about all
of them; explaining to me the meaning of
their gloomy rituals, their nervous, intricate
ways.

Anniversary of My Father's Death

For you, dad,
and also I guess for me,
I turn on the ballgame.

It doesn't matter
which game
exactly, does it?

So familiar, the way
you spent the long
hours
of your freedom,
soaking up
the drama, huge
warrior men in combat,
the thud of bodies, then
lifting themselves
out
of the mud. With
helmets off
on the sidelines, their
faces growing younger
year by year

We rooted
as if
it all mattered,
as if this

81

were the real
work of men as if
we were going
to live
forever and this
was the best
we could do,
watch.

At the end,
after the field goal
from
the 37 in
the final
seconds,
I can't
raise my hollow
male
body from the chair.

The Forest is Burning in the Palm of My Hand

My son comes running across acres of grass.
He is twenty-seven years old.
He is eleven years old. He is
four years old.

He turns his hand up to show me -
the distant inner glow, smoke
drifting from him.

He wants to see so I lift
my hands to the old paths
where fire often danced;
plateaus of desolation inside my fist.

My son comes running
across acres of grass.
He is four
years old. He
is eleven years old.
He is twenty-seven
years old.

Dreamless Night

— after years of fruitless psychotherapy

I hear the old mapmaker, Sigmund Freud,
calling out to me in his high-pitched voice:

>   "You have embarked on the wrong road.
>   That is not the royal route to the
>   unconscious I described."

And I, unaccountably,
keep wandering down this foolish
twisting gravel trail until I can no longer
hear his voice, and find myself alone,
high above the old river, quite
near the realm of silence.

From here, I won't observe the fierce
caravan of night:
                crossbearers and flagellants,
horsemen continuing their compulsive
hunt. I will miss the moment when
the lightning of God's wrath embeds itself
in an ancient oak, whose roots
absorb the blow like a woman wideopen
in childbirth, her hands gripping
each side of the bed.

Tonight I will know nothing - the inner
world hissing and struggling in the distance
like some huge, hungry torch.

It's too complicated to be a human being.
Everyone knows this somewhere
in their hearts. Taking our last breaths, six
problems will still torment us. Under
the heavy sands of our bodies, there is
a vast lake of thick oil smouldering
helplessly, that nonetheless runs our cells.

So Sigmund, if one night I fail to dream,
if I turn away from the road of self-knowledge,
let that stand as an offer of truce, a small
celebration, an acknowledgement
of complexity's limit, as when the traffic
halts, permitting the blind to cross.

Reflections on Samson

Selected Poems

Heart

The heart has medieval
persistence
and pumps out
blotchy tapestries
of thrones
and forests

to prove fidelity
it can chew up
mouthfuls
of stained glass
sending them
ringing into the blood
like a knight falling
from a turret

it never hesitates
it adores armor
it sustains the solemn beat
of the victor's horse
in the stone courtyard
of the vanquished

it is blind
and its burnt-out sockets stare
as in a starving face
at a dungeon window

yet it survives
the rack and the whip
only to kill itself
because the lady's body
is consumed
under another's hand

if allowed its own way
it will live for long periods
as an infant
yet it is also
the only one who can
locate the lost child
quicker than the wolves.

Nose

How powerful the nose began
like a trumpet blowing inward
and we followed its delicate roar
everywhere over the threatening ground

it blew the fire and smoke into our brains
and from it, close to the forest floor,
the knowledge of decay sank
into our hearts

we were like dogs then, not hesitating
to sniff the lovely, black acidity of
the genitals and also the scattered manure
of our own kind that told us we
were not alone

but then, as we struggled to stand up,
it was no longer decisive; it became
a joke, we came to overrule it, to pick
at it, to turn away from what it told us
of our own bodies

yet, even now at times, some surprising
perfume can resurrect the old trumpet
and it sounds again through our foreheads,
blows into the cheeks and causes the skull's
ancient stones to move

and we go down on our knees and crawl
forward, following the small general who
goes without pants, leading his naked
irregulars against the alien, beautiful armies
of uprightness.

Reflections on Samson

Samson turned up in Brooklyn
wearing a skin-diver's
outfit
and looking Caribbean.

They thought he was sent
by Fidel
and frisked him and suggested
he stay
out of the harbor muck.

Bur he was accustomed
to nothing
in this new world where
he needed tasks
worthy of his strength and
so walked for hours
asking advice from
the pigeons.

After some months he located
a mother and father
in Canarsie who spoke to him
in sign language. He learned
to eat very awkwardly
with a fork
and was encouraged

by the children to play baseball
which he mastered, but found
it hard to restrain the speed
of his pitch.

For a while he visited with
three girls -all small and pretty-
in the afternoons they would
swim in the harbor
leaping into the air
occasionally like dolphins.

When they called him for the draft
in 1965, he refused
at first, but later saw the chance
for heroism and served
as a nurse, carrying the wounded
out of range, one or
two under each arm.

Delilah was a rich girl
who had problems.
He went there often
to hear the piano and
argue with her father who
hated unions.

One day they bought him
a hat and a suit
and insisted he get his
hair cut.

After that he was never
the same. He woke up
tied to a desk, writing
articles for obscure
social science journals.

Of his several children
one was torn apart
by urges to be in two
places at once, of the others
there is no clear record.

Waking in the middle of the night after a dream

It fell through me
like a sudden rain

I caught some of it
in my hands

Now when I lift the water
to my mouth

I see it is made of drops
too large to swallow.

Evolution

I evolved
from
the ape

King
Kong storming
the Garden
of
Eden

and looking for
Eve

I had
a radical
heart that
misunderstood
sleep

a conservative sword
that
thought it
was a penis

a liberal
nose
that tolerated
anything

and now I
hunt hickory
nuts
like
an anarchist.

On the day my father would have been
62 years old

Everything has deepened

the bread of my hands
has grown wild, heavy shoots

I have stood sometimes
buried half-way in stones

dancing.

The Neurotic Man

He isn't
here.

He's a banker
stepping
into an elevator
who suddenly
goes deaf.

He's a boy
lying face down
in a ditch
while enemy planes
cruise
overhead.

But he knows
that on his wrists
strange hands
are growing
that belonged centuries
ago to a strangler.

Conjugation of the verb "to hope"

I hoped
— the night came anyway

I hoped
— the night came anyway

Is this the way to
do it?

No. Begin again.

I hoped,
today.

I will still hope,
tomorrow.

One day,
I will risk everything.

Abandoning the mechanical

— for my friends, the professors

It is sometimes this business
of having
to keep talking

I hear myself
making painful sounds
spinning and splattering
like a car
caught in the slush

I just want to
walk away, but I have
this fear
of needing to cover
so much desolate ground.

In memory of George Lewis, Great Jazzman

1

Man is the animal that knows
the clarinet

      makes his living
on the docks, a stevedore,
110 lbs., carrying what loads
he can

the Depression comes along,
his teeth rot, no money, and
he has to accept silence

2

Thirteen years
later
     they put the instrument
back together
       with rubber bands
bought him
new teeth
     and then he began

```
      I  C  E
   E           I
   C           C
   I           E
   C           C
   E           I
      I  C  E
C-------------------C

   R           R

    E           E

     A     A

      M  M
```

```
       E     R                    A    V
    V              T            W           E
 O                      H   E                   S
```

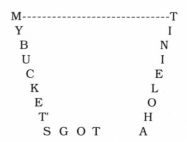

```
    M------------------------------T
    Y                              I
    B                              N
    U                              I
    C                              E
    K                              L
    E                              O
    T'                             H
      S  G  O  T        A
```

One song they say

       was pure
uninhibited joy
words
      cannot tell you

      survived so long
in those empty jaws

3

He lived and died
there.
Had a New Orleans funeral.

Leading the mourners
his old friends' band
trudged
      to the cemetery, heads
down, trombones scraping
the ground, slow tones of
"Just a Closer Walk..."
helping to carry
      the solemn mud
of their steps.

Graveside,
        words said, tears fallen,
they turned
        to walk back;
a few beats on the big
drum, then soft plucking
of a banjo string -
        in another block
the clarinet wailed
and then suddenly they were
playing
        "The Saints..." full blast
and people jumped
and shouted and danced
just as he'd known they would.

4

Alright. There is a frailness
in all our music.
Sometimes we're broken
and it's lost.
Sometimes we forget
for years it's even in us, heads
filled with burdens and smoke.

And sometimes we've held
to it and it's there,
waiting to break out
walking back from the end.

Freedom

Freedom looks like a bird
with long yellow
feathers

   I see it in the
tree near my house
It can't stay still
   It comes and goes
singing
and disappearing

I want to catch
it I call
to it

  Freedom! Freedom!

and find I am
  — however awkwardly —
flying

Parting

Wear the
        loose dress and

come down
to see me
        you know
the place
where
        the leaves

make the ground
reasonably
        soft

but it
doesn't matter
I'm going away

        take
the clip
out
        of your hair
say my name
and
        lie down
beside
me

      it's no good
I'm going away

wear
      the loose dress
and
come down
      and say my name
say my
name and
      lie beside
me
      while
I'm gone.

Mr. Love

— for my grandmother, Miss Reznikoff

You see, she explained, what is now
called Love, was once named Zaslovsky.

He lived over the delicatessen
talked Yiddish in his hoarse voice,
(the vocal cords strained from all
those years of singing)

argued some about politics, got
melancholy and often put the grand-

children to bed telling Russian stories.
He loved to play pinochle
      and never really gave up
his ideas.

But now, she explained, what
has taken the name of Love

fixes prescriptions, lives in
a perfect little neighborhood

and has plenty
      of acquaintances.

Empty

one pocket
no money
one pocket
the vague idea
from the dream

one pocket
the old forgotten stuff
one pocket
soaked, autumn, rain

I know I will find the cave dwellings
abandoned
I know I will come across myself
somewhere

pockets torn through
    begging entirely
at last

The Body

The body is not much

    — a black vase
with a thin neck — that
can't hold even
    three reeds

still, I've watched
my feet
    many times
and I've dreamed
    of hair that
the late sun
        passes through

and I've rocked
    in my body
like an infant
        in his father's arms
and like
a troubled man
    who begins to feel
the earth
    turning

and I'm stirred
    by the spectacle

of my fingers
　　　　each with its
dead end.

Thoughts on a line by Tuli Kupferberg

"to masturbate is human, to fuck divine."

I'd like to learn three lessons about
the body
and three lessons about the mind.

I'd like to forget nothing
and start all over

I'd like to catch you from behind

I'd like to be taken in by the thighs
that bind, pretty tight

I'd like to learn six lessons about
the body
and six lessons about the mind.

I'd like to see what
I can't find

I'd like to go far right here

I'd like to catch you from behind

I'd like to know what
was designed

I'd like to learn six lessons about
the body
and six lessons about the mind

I'd like to be kind,
appropriately

I'd like to know what
was designed

I'd like to catch you from behind.

Certain Poems

Certain poems twist
    over and over and
fly like rocks
    thrown down from
a mountain
in Korea

in my pocket
I've got
    50 (count them!)
50
    but you don't go for their
furry hats and
untrimmed beards. Too
religious
    you say.

Flying, you say,
they look
like
    remnants of meteors
pock-marked
and eaten away by acid rain

I take them
lovingly
    in my hands
      — see this smooth one —

it glides
over the lake humming
mountain tunes

I get down on
my knees and pour
them on the ground
& while
you look they
begin
to trudge away,
old, dark
elves.

The Neurotic Woman

— for J. with agoraphobia

She can't go anywhere. She can't
get in the car and drive off
a cliff
    She chains herself to the house
and thinks: "Today I suffered for how many
minutes?"
    Then she turns away from herself
like a bystander from the first blood
of an accident.

She finds herself hating the trees.
They carry on just the same; hard-
working, bourgeois trees - dragging
up drops of water into roots, clasping
the sun greedily like a bankbook,
drinking and sunning themselves just
to stay alive.
    How easy for them building
up their little savings accounts. "O
boring nature, I wish I could just punch
your clock!"

And certain problems: the long hours
of the night, the stomach that speaks its
as yet untranslatable language, the
jewel thief sense of squeezing by and
hiding. One gets weary of scrounging

for a meaning in the cracks like
a spiritual rat.

But it's the faces of her children
she cannot stand; their heavy, demanding
faces; their determined weight of sandbags
piled high to keep her from escaping, to
keep her from flooding wildly over everything.
What unbearable joy
        to see them waiting for a wet
embrace.

At the doctor's she is supposed to learn
to cry out.
        But for every sound
a village must be burned somewhere
far back in the interior;
      burned to the ground
the way the Cossacks did it,
           the Jews fleeing
into the forest.
Later, as they throw water
on the flames
      she must emerge from
her hiding place
like a spirit the fire set free
      and greet them all
and tell them her
        strange new name.

Cold Water

Selected Poems

Cold Water

Cold water on my bare feet.
You are like cold water.

All day I've watched the water
run from the tap, splash into the bushes
where the earth awaits it
and sucks it up.

Cold water! the grass exclaims.

To A Fighter Killed in the Ring

In a gym in Spanish Harlem
boys with the eyes of starved leopards
flick jabs at your ghost
chained to a sandbag.

They smell in the air the brief truth of poverty
just as you once did:
                    "The weak don't get rich."

                * * * * * * * * *

You made good.
Probably you were a bastard,
dreaming of running men down in a Cadillac
and tearing blouses off women.

And maybe in your dreams great black teeth
ran after you down deadend alleyways
and the walls of your room
seemed about to collapse,
bringing with them a sky of garbage
and your father's leather strap.
And you sat up afraid you were dying
just as you had so many nights as a child.

                * * * * * * * * *

Small bruises to the brain.
An accumulation
of years of being hit.

I will not forget that picture of you
hanging over the ropes, eyes closed,
completely wiped out.
Like a voice lost in the racket
of a subway train
roaring on under the tenements of Harlem.

Skinny Poem

Skinny
poem,
all
your
ribs
showing
even
without
a
deep
breath

thin
legs
rotted
with
disease

Live
here!
on
this
page,
barely
making
it
like
the
mass
of
mankind.

Prospect Beach

Here I slept with my face turned
        toward the sun,
my eyes closed and my arms lying
        beside me
like two different animals that
        enjoyed my smell.

What roar, ocean! What an alien
        you are.
You are clear and indecipherable
        and full of fish:
strange and fast ones; and full
        of wild plants.

I watched the striped killies
        swim near shore
and the children splashing about
        holding glass jars;
trying to catch a fish
        in a bare hand.

And I was old, with the taste of sleep
        in my mouth.
Old and solitary, shivering
        in the breeze.
there are none like me here, only
        companions and marvels.

After Visiting a Home for Disturbed Children

Broken lamps!
Their faces shine with a destroyed light:
illumination
of tangled gestures, of silent beatings,
of the black river of childhood.
Terrible light.

A light to which I cannot speak.
Light of corroding marriages.
Light of secret cries lost
like the signals of minute stars.
Light of empty basements
in which children have carefully hidden their names.

At night, unable to sleep, I stare
out the window at the empty road
and bits of light shine out of the dark -
intense, searching,
like the eyes of a girl who is buried alive.

Why I Left My Job in a Garment Factory

Wings!
Mouth!
     Eyes!
Cock!

     Where are you?

Is this the best we can do? this dust
this dark factory I hate
the soaped-up windows,
100,000 skirts hanging
on iron bars over my head?

Lunch hour when we collapse
or play cards and curse management?

Monotony and sad visions of
plaid skirts turning into teenage girls naked
only from the waist up?

Aren't we poets? Haven't we demanded
"to each according to his need?"
I need to take off my shoes and
get loved.

Winter Twilight

over the dark highway,
over the woods
and the clusters of small houses,
the clouds appear

----- the great clouds of a winter twilight!

    when i see them i feel like a hundred men
    who have slipped out of prison without
    a trace

the great clouds -------

    ragged and ancient like the heart,
    like the heads of old, pious men
    we cannot help loving

and everything that was forgotten takes
hold of me
i walk out into the small congregation
of the twilight
and find i must sing and weep and
speak to the dead.

City Summer

Things come out.

After lunch, a young guy
in an undershirt
pisses into a pile of worn tires,
whistling.

Above the clinging adolescents
in the dark street,
an old lady watches from her window
like a deposed princess
despising the revolution.

Under the trees
I fall on Helen by surprise
like a caterpillar.

A Task

— reply to Auden & the intellectuals

Potatoes. I will hunt potatoes
in the fashion of my grandmother
who fed us all.

Potatoes. Like the tough hearts of young men.
The core of dark joy in sexual love.
The world that trembles and changes.

In the fashion of my grandmother
I will abandon all exotic things

and hunt a language
of odd, true shapes that were nurtured in the old earth.

For a Teacher of Disturbed Children

— for Pat

With the slashed eyes of their imprisonment
they tear off your toes.
But you never move,
as if there were roots in the soles of your feet.

Their impassable memories, like washed-out bridges,
overwhelm your air with brown water.
Their rigid faces, stolen from murderers waiting to die,
turn your movement into stones.

You stand stripped and tall:
        a tree whose limbs have been broken by armless
boys.

But you grow again:
send out new leaves and branches.
You wrap their pained eyes and their sores in your color.

You see the mind emerge from its agony,
slowly, like a sapling from the shackles of a rocky earth.
Then in place of crimes there is a world.

The Feeding

We sit in the darkness
and the baby drinks from you.
Alive! I can't
believe it.

We are silent. Far off,
great explosives
stand in hundreds of holes
sucked out of the planet;
millions of men
who might have befriended each other
prowl the earth's surface
as hunters.

You open your eyes
and look at me
and I see you are satisfied.
The baby sleeps.
You have nourished what you can,
which is no small triumph
in a starved time.

Sleep

I have a vision
of the entire world asleep.
Wonderful, undisturbed sleep --
the way I sleep on a winter morning.

I see millions of poor men
whose hearts are tired,
lying quietly
close to the cool surface
of the earth.

I see the leaders of nations
in the fantastic houses of state,
mouths open on their pillows.

In the area
of delivery systems,
technicians sleep underground.
And in many places I see soldiers
in their underwear,
sleeping one-by-one
on millions of cots.

And everyone is dreaming
of his childhood;
dreaming of a darkness
he cannot understand,
of old games and faces he had forgotten.

and no one stirs
and no one is
under orders.

Thaw in the City

Now my legs begin to walk.
The filthy piles of snow are melting.
Pavements are wet.

What clear, tiny streams!
Suddenly I feel the blood flowing in the veins
in the backs of my hands.

And I hear a voice -a wonderful voice-
as if someone I loved and forgot had lifted
a window and called my name.

The streets wash over me like waves.
I sail in the boat of sidewalks and sparrows
out of sight.

The Night

Like old shadows,
highways of diseased moonlight
like an ancient sore
torn out of the sky,
the night begins to enter us.

And within nerves there is a stirring of strange boots.
Silently, in the blackness, a rifleman
smelling of decay knocks on the door of his room
untouched since World War II.

On a dark stairway, a man stares into abandoned
apartments looking for his father's praise.
Slowly, the mind opens and blood vessels
reach out like huge trees,
touching the hours.

Alone. Across the great distance of dreams
men cannot help each other.
And there is that silence ---
as if a mute were dragged under by the sea.

Willimantic, Conn.

A company spokesman
has denied
the rumor
that all men are sailors.

He has explained
that the desert is loved
by personnel
and that employees
are naturally attracted
to machine dust.
He said that clerks
were part of the caravan
of blank eyes.

As for strange dreams
of ships
and impossible fish,
he said they were a direct consequence
of wetting the lips
too often.

Remedy for a Guy who's Sick of his Line of Work

Beautiful labor, man! That's
what we need.
The dark, lovely work that's done in dreams
where nothing is clear;
as its done invisibly
in roots of trees.

Forget about necessities.
Walk elsewhere. Hat off.
Ready to be rained on.
Hunched over, jubilant,
as if your legs were translating the lines
of an unknown poet.

A Road

Dead ones, there is a road
without tree
without cornfield
      a dry road
      of small stones
a bare road

I will walk to you
as a blind man crossing the continent
carrying only his wits

Dead ones, there is your ocean
on a bare road.

It is time I stood there:
a blind man
facing the sad noise of the waves

      without tree
      without cornfield

For kayak magazine

Our words are no steadier than our journeys
than the marriage collapsing
like a drunk at the wheel at 90 mph.

Our poems, full of halts, emergencies, far-off lights,
indecipherable smells, blind alleys,
I cannot apologize for them.
They are no worse than the thick traffic jam of losses
we are stuck in.

Our poems, shining and deadly, dense with emptiness
represent the dark interior
-----hearts of multitudes like factories at night
full of silent, black machinery and the smell of oil.

But, our poems also rave at dusk. burn secretly in fields
- mad, nativistic,
like hope's Ku Klux Klan obsessed with reconstruction.

For B., with the blues

"You ever been down you know how I feel
— feel like an engine ain't got no drivin' wheel."
Brownie McGhee

When I hear George Lewis blowing
his clarinet
when I listen to Kid Shots, Slow Drag
and the others beating it out -
when I listen to this old jazz
I think it's not too late! Still
there is something to grab onto -
the small purple flowers
still make it to the surface.

The wild and gentle survive
somewhat.
Things still open -
turn outward -
doors, hands, eyes,
the light
of human bodies.

Strange joy!
In the harsh dark,
the cock can crow, sweetly,
between legs.

A Note

Look! in the bowl on your dresser I've put

    daffodils
       and clover

    They will be my eyes
to watch over you in the difficult night.

And I am taking a blackness from your hair.
I want to feel its warmth
as I ride the road among worn and nervous
men.

Return

No moon.
My boots crunch on the iced-over path.
The woods are still
I have nowhere to go.

Then from some place
you jump out and throw yourself
on my shoulders.
You've come back.

I will carry you,
strange rider.

Drunk, two afternoons

Drunk, two afternoons.
I am a tree gone mad because my tangled roots
have finally touched sweet water.

In the evening along the path from her house
I am crazed with joy.
Her eyes sail in my veins like small, black fish
in a narrow stream.

O I will stay here forever
growing higher
with snow in my hair.

Night Train

A flash of cobalt over the railroad crossing —
it gleams like a well-kept pistol
beside the delicate ear of a sleeping town.

The hard earth shakes and crumbles
as under the feet of a long army.
In his bed, a man sits up frightened,
sure he has heard something.

Probably the locomotive whistle —
or maybe this the arrival
of that deep, intricate destruction
of which we all claim innocence.

Reading a Poem by Walt Whitman I Discover
We Are Surrounded by Companions

Reading Walt Whitman, I find he compares his soul to a
      spider.
      Fantastic! Who could know he would?

And suddenly, my life tips over! a bed in a rat-infested
      apartment, scared kids jumping on one end.

My head can take it — like a cheap flowerpot with
hyacinths uncracked after a four-story drop

My heart, that was just a heart, begins
to fit everywhere, like newspapers
stuffed into the cracked ceilings on 125th street.

Political Poem, after Neruda, 1965

"Once crime was solitary as a cry of protest;
now it is as universal as science."
Albert Camus

Behind me I hear the sad commands
of confused military.
From a window over my head
come the edicts of the legislature of madness,
no longer able to keep itself secret.

I am running down an alley of filthy centuries;
of lies implacable as gravity.
I hear ordinary people, turned into executioners,
rejoicing in their victories.
I see a woman's hand rusting like a mineral
in the pathetic formations of politics.
I watch typhoons of longing and bewilderment
growing in the brains of children.

Behind every dream stands a battalion of deranged bones.

And I see that none of us
will ever enter the warm mouth of the sea.
We will never meet the delicate animals
of authentic tenderness, or the silver
children of felicities.

We will never enter the great structure
of clear eyes that lives
in the cells of our hands.

Tonight, as always, men sleep
but nations are awake.
Loneliness drifts across the landscape
like gas. Plans are made
and many are dying. Like a shell fragment,
sorrow rips open the skull.
And my eyes, two wanderers seeking shelter,
continue their journey
through the time of detonations and losses.

Evening

At the bus stop
            a man
            I know
tries
        to wipe off
        the heavy dust
that has
fallen
        on him

            with this rag
        of a poem.

The Author

Lou Lipsitz has a diverse history. As a poet, he has published two previous books — *Cold Water* (Wesleyan Press, 1967) and *Reflections on Samson* (kayak press, 1977). His work appears in numerous anthologies and is widely used in teaching poetry in public schools. His writing has been influenced by the American poets Robert Bly, Galway Kinnell, Denise Levertov, Gary Snyder, and James Wright, but also shaped by non-English language poets including Pablo Neruda, Zbigniew Herbert, and Rolf Jacobsen. Currently a psychotherapist in Chapel Hill, NC with a strong focus on men's issues, he was for thirty years previous a professor of political science at the University of North Carolina. He taught democratic theory and political psychology and was the author of a widely used text in American politics and of numerous scholarly articles. Lipsitz' involvement in the men's movement over the last ten years has markedly affected his writing. In his new book, *Seeking the Hook*, many of the poems are closely related to such issues, including father/child relationships, struggling with anger and grief, finding the "deep masculine" in oneself, and forming stronger bonds with other men.

Lipsitz was born in Brooklyn, NY in 1938. He is divorced, and has two children and two grandchildren.